BASKETBALL

Contents

Published by Heinemann Library
an imprint of Heinemann Publishers (Oxford) Ltd
Halley Court, Jordan Hill, Oxford OX2 8EJ

OXFORD LONDON EDINBURGH MADRID
ATHENS BOLOGNA PARIS MELBOURNE
SYDNEY AUCKLAND SINGAPORE TOKYO
IBADAN NAIROBI HARARE GABORONE
PORTSMOUTH NH (USA)

© 1994 Heinemann Library

98 97 96 95
10 9 8 7 6 5 4 3 2

ISBN 0 431 07431 3

Designed by Ron Kamen, Green Door Design Ltd, Basingstoke,
England

Illustrated by Barry Atkinson

British Library Cataloguing in Publication Data
Marshall, David
  Basketball. – (Successful Sports Series)
  I. Title II. Series
  796.323

Printed in China

Acknowledgements

The Publishers would like to thank the
following for permission to reproduce
photographs:

Action-plus: pp. 24, 28; Allsport:
imprint, pp. 1, 4, 6, 7, 11, 13, 20, 26,
27; The Basketball Association: p. 16;
Colorsport: pp. 5, 10, 12, 17, 29;
Northampton Mercury: p.25; Meg
Sullivan and Andrew Waters: pp. 3,
8 (left and right), 9, 14, 15, 18, 19.

Cover photograph © Action-plus

Thanks to the C. J. Worcester,
member of the Basketball
National Coaching Committee
and co-author of the *Basketball
Curriculum Guide*, for his
comments on the manuscript.

The Publishers have made every
effort to trace copyright holders.
However, if any material has been
incorrectly acknowledged, we would
be pleased to correct this at the
earliest opportunity.

Introduction

The commentators were tremendously excited. Their voices got louder and faster...

*'I was hugely impressed with his **lay-up** shots in the first few minutes. Six baskets in just a few minutes. But that was nothing compared to what we have just seen. Have you ever seen such amazing one- and two-handed **dunks**?'*

*'Never in my whole sports-watching career! And don't forget his amazing **hook-shots** close to half-time, and seven out of seven foul shots. Now the whole team seems to be inspired.'*

Lay-ups? Dunks? Hook-shots? Foul shots? They can only be describing one game: basketball.

Basketball has come a long way from the simple game invented in 1892 by Dr James A. Naismith at a YMCA (Young Men's Christian Association) training school in Springfield, Massachusetts, USA. He was worried because very few members of the club were turning up for his indoor practice sessions when the weather was too bad for them to be outside. He nailed two peach-baskets on the balconies at each end of the gym, and told his students to run and see if they could throw a ball into them. Because the gym floor was so hard, and because he wanted to avoid accidents, Naismith made up rules that stopped the students from touching each other as they ran. Basketball was born. The only problem was that every time someone scored they had to climb up a ladder and get the ball out of the basket. A little while later they decided that the game was more important than carrying peaches, and cut the bottoms out of the baskets.

Ron Curry scores a basket during this game between Russia and Bulgaria.

Playing the game

Basketball is usually played indoors on a rectangular court. The playing surface is made of wood or rubber. Practice games are often played outdoors. In America it is played almost anywhere a piece of hard ground is available. At each end of the court is the target, called a basket, a metal hoop high above the ground. The hoop has a loose string net hanging from it, and it is fixed to a backboard. The hoop is 3 m (10 ft) above the ground. The court is 28.6 m (94 ft) long and 14 m (46 ft) wide. The object of the game is to put the ball in the opponents' basket and so score points.

The ball is round and slightly bigger than a football and weighs a lot more – around 650 grams (23 ounces). The ball is not smooth, but has a grainy surface that makes it easier to hold.

At each end of the court there is an area below the basket marked in the shape of a keyhole. This is called the **key** or the **three-second area**. Most scores are made from this area. At the end of the key area, 4.6 m (15 ft) from the basket, is the **free-throw line**, used for taking **free-throws** or foul shots.

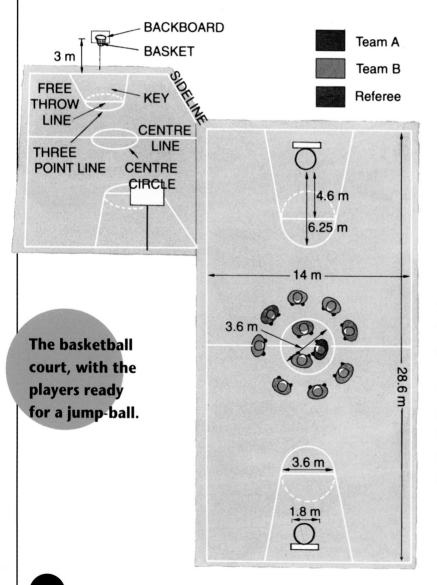

BACKBOARD
BASKET
3 m
FREE THROW LINE
KEY
SIDELINE
CENTRE LINE
THREE POINT LINE
CENTRE CIRCLE

Team A
Team B
Referee

4.6 m
6.25 m
14 m
3.6 m
28.6 m
3.6 m
1.8 m

The basketball court, with the players ready for a jump-ball.

There is an arc on the court around the basket 6.25 m (21 ft) from under the centre of the basket. This is known as the **three-point line** (see page 5).

A jump-ball.

Across the middle of the court is the **centre line**. In the middle of this is the **centre circle**, which is 3.6 m (12 ft) across. The game is started from within this circle.

Apart from the court with its baskets, backboards and lines there are no special requirements for playing basketball. Starters at the game need only have a pair of training shoes and PE kit. Players can try to protect their elbows and knees with soft padding but this is not usually done and no other protection is allowed. Because of the speed and frantic nature of the game, any other clothing would just be a nuisance.

Professional or club players have to wear matching vests and shorts. Each player must have a number on the front and back of their vest. Players on international teams use numbers from 4 to 15; otherwise numbers are usually in groups, for instance 20 to 25, 30 to 35 and so on.

Both halves of the game are started with a **jump-ball**. At the centre circle the referee throws the ball up and a player from each team jumps up and tries to tip the ball to one of his or her own team mates.

The game, the teams and scoring points

There are ten players in a basketball team, but only five players from each team are actually on the court at the same time. A full game lasts for 40 minutes, made up of two halves of 20 minutes each. The professional game, however, has four quarters of twelve minutes each. Every time the **referee** blows the whistle the clock is stopped. This means that a game can actually last for an hour and a half, including the half-time break.

It is impossible to have a tie or draw in basketball. If the scores are level at the end of 40 minutes an extra five minutes are played. If the scores are still tied then five more minutes are added, and so on, until there is a result.

One of the reasons basketball is such an exciting game is that the players are always moving and passing or **dribbling** the ball. The main cause of this non-stop action is the many rules about time limits.

Once a team has the ball and is on the attack it must make a shot on the basket within 30 seconds (or 24 seconds in the professional game); if it fails to shoot in that time then the other team is given the ball to start an attack from the side-line. Also, when a team has scored then the other team must restart the game from its end-line within five seconds.

Derrick McKey taking a shot for the Sonics.

It has ten seconds to move the ball over the centre line. If it fails then possession is given to the other team. Once past the centre line, the attacking team cannot pass or dribble the ball back over the line.

No player on the attacking team can stay in the key area for more than three seconds, which is why it is also called the three-second area. These time limits mean that the game is fast and free-moving. In most other sports or games it is possible to take a breather now and then. In basketball it is impossible even to stand still! A player is always involved. It also means that it is unusual for a player to stay on court for the whole 40 minutes of a game. One way a team coach can give players a break is by calling a **time-out**, which can last up to a minute. Each team can call two time-outs per half. These give the coach time to change the team's tactics or ask about a player's fitness. The time-out can also break up the play and take the pressure off a losing team.

Pointers

Stay alert after you have scored a basket. You feel really good when you have just scored, and might stop concentrating. In that time the other team may well score.

Every time a player shoots the ball into the basket during play, the player's team gets two points, or three if the shot is made from outside the three-point line. The ball must go through the hoop from the top and can be rebounded in off the backboard. If a player is fouled then he or she will be awarded a free throw. These are taken from the free-throw line, and if the throw results in a score the player's team will be awarded one point.

Positions

There are three main positions in basketball: **guards**, **forwards** and **centres** (sometimes called posts or pivots). Everyone in the team must be able to pass, shoot and defend. None of the players have fixed positions on court.

The guards are usually the smaller, quicker members of the team. They must be able to dribble, pass the ball well and shoot from a long range. The guards control what the team is doing. They set up attacks and slow or speed up the play. They nearly always play further away from the basket and, therefore, must be good long-range shooters. When a team has two guards on the court one will be a good ball-handler and passer, and the other will be a good shooter.

Alton Byrd, playing here for Manchester, is a short player in basketball terms.

The forwards are usually taller than the guards and normally play on either side of the key area. These players must be good shooters, particularly from the side of the court. They should also be good passers because they are often the link to the centres.

BASKETBALL FACTS

The first great centre in American basketball was Bill Russell. He set the standard by which all other exceptionally tall players have since been judged. He was 2.08 m (6 ft 10 in) tall and very agile, and the outstanding professional player of the 1960s. At the age of 32, in 1966, he became the first black coach of any major professional United States sports team when he was signed by the Boston Celtics.

The other players are the giants of the game. The centres are the tallest players in the team and play close to the basket where they can use their height to the best advantage. They not only have to be able to score, but they are expected to defend the other basket as well. Another benefit from their height is that their long legs can get them from one end of the court to the other in no time!

Magic Johnson is tall by anyone's standards!

Throwing and passing

Once a player has the ball he or she must try to move it forwards to score in the opponent's basket. When the ball is caught the player must begin to bounce the ball with one hand within five seconds if closely marked, or the player must pass or shoot. Everyone in the team has to be good at passing and shooting.

The **chest pass** is the most important and basic pass in the game, and is used for fast, accurate passes over short distances. The ball is held in both hands close to the chest. As the picture shows, the ball is then passed by shooting the arms forward to their full extent and pushing the ball with the wrists and fingers.

Tall players often use the **two-hand overhead pass** to go over the top of shorter players. The ball is held over the head and flicked with the fingers and wrists to a team mate. When managed successfully, it is the best pass of all because it can completely change the direction of play.

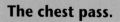
The chest pass.

The bounce pass is easy to intercept.

A **hand-off pass** is a very short pass between two players running close to each other. As one player runs across a team mate, the ball is tossed in the air for the other to catch.

A **bounce pass** is when the ball is sent from one player to another by bouncing it between them. It is often used to get under a tall player. This pass is slower, and more likely to fail than any other. There are too many players on the court, all moving about at speed, for a bounce pass to be really safe.

Any two players on the court can take part in the fast, attacking part of the game called 'give and go'. When a player has given a pass, he or she should immediately move forwards, looking to receive a return pass. Defending players often look to see where the ball has gone when a pass is made. This gives their opponents a few valuable seconds to get into a good position to take the return pass. This is the most common attacking method and should be practised at all training sessions.

A two-hand overhead pass can change the direction of play.

Dribbling

The dribble is the most exciting and most difficult of all basketball skills. It is also an important skill because the only way you can keep the ball is by dribbling it. To dribble, the player must take the ball after a pass with one hand and start to move immediately. It is very tempting to bounce the ball just once after you have caught it, but if you do, you cannot have another dribble once you have stopped.

In the dribble a player moves, pushing the ball down to the ground. The ball is bounced with the fingers, by flicking the wrist and fingers. You should not use the flat palm of your hand because you need to feel and move the ball as you go. Dribbling should be practised so that movement can be made by touch only – you should not have to look at the ball. You must be able to look and see where your team mates and the basket are when you are dribbling.

Pointers

It is important to practise so that you can dribble equally well with both hands. This will mean that you can change direction and speed at any time. If you can only dribble with one hand it will be easy for a defender to force you away from the basket.

Dribbling the ball towards the basket to beat an opponent and take a shot is called a **drive**. Players will drive towards opponents to try to force them to make mistakes. Defenders must stand their ground. A common mistake for defenders facing good dribblers is to move towards them. The defenders would then be off-balance and easy for a good dribbler to beat. If a dribbler looks as though he or she is going to shoot, the defender may jump to block the shot. However, it may be a trick and the dribbler will be able to move forwards as the defender is still in the air.

The defender should not act too soon since the rules of the game make it the duty of the dribbler to keep out of contact with the defenders (see pages 14 and 15).

No one will wait and give you time to change direction, or stop and shoot, when you have been dribbling. That is why you must practise dribbling – or try passing instead.

Excellent dribbling skills at the Seoul Olympics in 1988.

John Stockton dribbling expertly.

When the dribbler has the ball and is moving forwards he or she must make sure to dribble around players who are in the way or else to trick them into jumping or moving the wrong way. If there is a collision in the process, the dribbler will be penalized.

Shooting

Shooting at the basket is undoubtedly the most popular part of basketball – everyone likes to score. The two forwards and the centre do most of the shooting. They are usually the tallest players in the team. The guards should practise taking long-range shots and lay-ups at speed.

Having caught the ball, a player should check to see whether or not it is possible to score. If the basket is not in view, he

Charles Barkley, supported by Larry Bird, takes a shot at the basket.

or she must be able to turn on one foot – a pivot – to look for the basket. If there is space to move forward when facing the basket, the player could dribble in and take a lay-up shot. This is a shot taken at the basket while on the run. The player moves quickly towards the basket, jumps up, and lays the ball on to the basket, or the backboard, at full stretch with one hand. Because this takes speed and height it is a spectacular move. These shots are often missed by inexperienced players. The ball will often rebound from the backboard. Really tall players can jump so high they can put the ball into the basket. They often throw the ball down into the basket from above. This is a called a dunk shot and is enjoyed by everyone, except perhaps the defending team.

The **jump-shot** is the most common, and most effective, shot in the professional game. It is taken from a standing position or at the end of a dribble, close to the basket. The player tries to take off vertically using both feet. As he or she jumps the ball is moved from in front of the face to a point just above the head. From there it is shot towards the basket with a flick of the wrist and fingers.

If the ball misses the basket from a lay-up, or jump shot, then it will often bounce off the backboard and into play. The tall centres and forwards will be under the basket and will try to regain possession. This is called taking a rebound. If the attacking team takes the rebound then it should try to shoot straight away.

The **set shot** is the easiest to practise but the least useful in open play. It is the shot used by forwards and guards when they are a long way away from the basket. A player prepares for the shot, with feet apart and knees slightly bent, before launching the ball towards the basket with an extended arm and a flick of the wrist and fingers. It is the shot used when taking free throws after a foul has been committed.

The hook-shot is the most difficult shot in the game and should not be used by inexperienced players. The idea is to run and jump or step towards the basket. The ball is held low and is brought round from behind the body in a long, looping throw and hooked towards the basket at arms' length. It is a shot that is very spectacular when it works, but it can look terrible and give the ball away if it does not work.

Personal fouls

Ever since James Naismith invented the game, basketball has been a non-contact sport. This means that players are not supposed to touch each other during the game. Therefore any time a player bumps into another it could be called a foul – and it usually is. Although players get very excited, as do the crowds, they must keep their tempers under control and avoid pushing, pulling, bumping, holding, tripping or charging an opponent. All these are **personal fouls**.

A personal foul – pushing.

A personal foul can be one of several different types. It can be a common foul, which is not obvious or intentional; a double foul, in which two players on opposite sides commit personal fouls against each other at about the same time; or a multiple foul, where two players on one team foul an opponent at the same time.

When the referee or **umpire** calls a player for a foul the player must raise his or her hand and face the scorer's table. This shows that the players know they have been penalized. The referee signals the player's number to the scorers' table and the foul is noted against the player's name on the score-sheet.

A multiple foul.

Pointers

If a personal foul has been committed against you and you have been knocked over or pushed around, it is a good idea to go off and have a break. If you stay on you may be at less than full speed, or angry, and less effective for your team.

Any player who commits five personal fouls in a game will be told to leave the court and will not be allowed to take part in that game any more. This is called being fouled-out. The coach is allowed to send on another player as a replacement. In the American professional game it takes six fouls before a player is fouled-out.

When a player is called for a personal foul, the foul is also marked against the team. When a team reaches its limit – in the professional game this amounts to four fouls a quarter, but in most games it is seven fouls per half – the opposing team gets extra free throws (see page 18).

Violations and technical fouls

Teams and players can also break the rules by committing **violations** and **technical fouls**. These are more difficult for the referee and umpire to spot than personal fouls are.

Violations include: running or walking with the ball without dribbling; double-dribbling (using both hands to dribble); holding the ball for more than five seconds and not passing to a team mate; and goaltending (stopping the ball on its downward path into the basket). Other violations are kicking or punching the ball. Breaking any of the time limits is also a violation (see pages 4 and 5).

After a violation, the opposing team is given the ball on the side-line to throw back into play, at a point nearest the spot where the offence happened. A team also loses possession of the ball if it lets the ball go off the court. The other team then brings the ball back into play from the point where the ball went out.

Throw in from the side-line.

Most technical fouls are against what is called 'the spirit of the game'. This means that a team has spoiled the way that the game is being played. Technical fouls can be committed by players on or off the court, or even by coaches and spectators! Technical fouls are called against players and teams for delaying a game, unfair conduct, illegal substitutions or illegal time-outs (see page 5). Free throws can be awarded after technical fouls.

In 1987 an American inter-college game was held up for several minutes when a dog got onto the court. No one was quite sure where it came from. During the break in play one of the centres, who had been injured earlier, received extensive treatment and was able to carry on. His team won the game. No one thought about the incident any more until a few weeks later when the other centre in one of the teams involved in the 'dog' game was injured and the same dog appeared on the court. The coach of the other team remembered reading about the other dog incident and called his opponents for a technical foul. After some discussion the call was allowed. The college team were told to get rid of their dog!

Everyone is near the action, and even those not on court get involved in the game – especially the coach.

Held ball and free throws

Sometimes a player from each team reaches for the ball at the same time and both end up holding it. This is called a **held ball**. If the ball does not shake free straight away, or if the referee is unable to decide who should be given the ball, then the game is stopped. The referee then restarts the game with a jump-ball between the two players involved.

If a player has been fouled then he or she is awarded one or more free throws. If the player was in the act of shooting and a basket is scored then the points will stand and the player will get one free throw. If the foul stopped a score being made then two or three free throws will be awarded. Every free throw is taken from the free-throw line and is worth one point. A player has five seconds to take each free throw. When a free throw is being taken none of the other players can go into the key area.

When two players end up holding the ball, it is called a held ball.

The leading free-throw expert in the history of the National Basketball Association (NBA) American League is Moses Malone who scored with 8395 attempts. The best free-thrower though was Dolph Schayes who scored with 6979 attempts out of 8273. This means he scored 17 times out of every 20 free-throws he made.

If a player has committed a technical foul then the other team is given two free throws. The captain must say who is to take the throws. If the technical foul is committed by the non-playing members of the team or the team coach then two free throws are awarded to the other team. When these throws have been taken the game is restarted from the side at the centre line by the free-throwing team.

Free throws are taken using the set-shot method. They are the easiest way of scoring points and all players should practise them so that they are seldom missed.

Taking a free throw.

The scorer and scoring

The only way to score points is by putting the ball into the basket, for one, two or three points. Because the game is so fast the jobs of the scorer and the time-keeper are perhaps the most difficult of all the officials. The scorer normally sits at a table and has an official score-sheet, a signal (a horn or bell) and five markers, numbered one to five. The names and numbers of all the players taking part are written down. This means the scorer can show the number of fouls committed to the players, coaches, umpire and referee.

As the game progresses a running total of the points scored by each team and a note of all personal fouls committed by players are kept by the scorer. When there is a total of five fouls against any player, or seven against a team, the scorer must show this to the referee or umpire. The number of fouls committed by each player is shown by raising a marker. The scorer also sounds the signal to indicate when a time-out has been taken.

The scoreboard displays all the important information about the game going on.

Very few professional players become time-keepers when they stop playing. They say it is irritating and too complicated. When you are a time-keeper there is no time to admire the game and applaud. You have to ignore how good a player is and keep watching and recording what is going on!

The score-sheet consists of three sheets on top of each other. In competition the top copy (white) is for the organizers of the game; the second copy (pink) is for the winning team; the bottom copy (gold) is for the losing team.

As you can see from the score-sheet below, the sheet is divided into sections, each of which is split into five columns. The middle column (M) shows the minutes of the game, and is numbered from 1 to 20 for the minutes in each half. The score for each team is shown in the other columns, the two to the right for the team attacking the right-hand basket, and the others for the team attacking the left. To distinguish the teams from each other the scorer calls one A and the other B. At half-time the sections of the sheet are reversed. The score-sheet also shows how many fouls have been committed by each team and each player. When you remember how simple the game is to play, it seems a very complicated game to score!

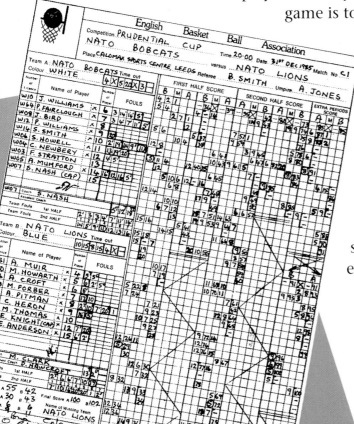

Using two stop-watches, a game watch and a time-out watch, the time-keeper has to check the length of time-outs. He or she has to stop the clock and restart it whenever there is a break in the game. Using a different signal the time-keeper stops the game at the end of each half.

This is an actual score-sheet – you can see how complicated it is.

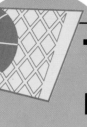

The umpire and the referee

In competition there are two officials who are jointly in charge: the referee and the umpire. Their main aim is to keep the game moving as much as possible. They will only stop the action by blowing their whistle when they have to. When they have stopped the game they need to show why by using one of the many official signals.

The referee is the senior official and is responsible for inspecting the ball and court before, and, if necessary, during the game. The referee tosses the ball to start the game and examines the score-sheet at half-time and at the end to approve the score. If the umpire and referee disagree on whether a basket counts or not, the referee makes the final decision.

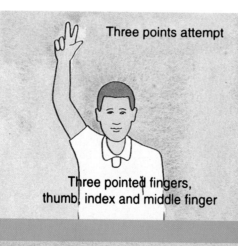

Three points attempt

Three pointed fingers, thumb, index and middle finger

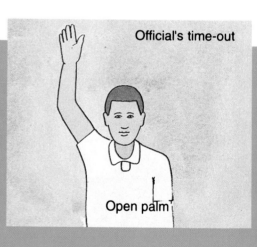

Official's time-out

Open palm

These are some of the signals that the officials make during a game.

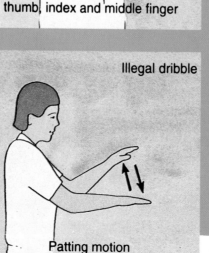

Illegal dribble

Patting motion

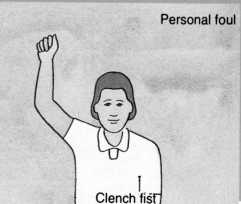

Personal foul

Clench fist

Either the referee or the umpire puts the ball back into play, stops play when the ball is dead, awards a time-out, allows substitutes onto the court, and keeps an eye on the time-keeper in order to judge on technical fouls.

The referee and the umpire control the game by dividing up their duties. They keep off the court as much as they can. They usually take responsibility for the side-line nearest them and the end-line to their right, as they face the court. During the course of a game neither official tries to keep up with the ball as it moves from end to end. This would be both exhausting and impossible. They try to keep one official ahead of the play (the leading official) and one behind the play (the trailing official). Either will blow a whistle for fouls committed anywhere on the court.

Technical foul
'T' form with palm showing

Intentional foul
Grasp wrist

Illegal use of hands
Strike wrist

Three free throws
Thumb, index and middle finger pointed on both hands

Famous players

In a poll taken in the USA in 1993, the basketball player Michael Jordan was voted the world's greatest athlete. He dominated the professional game since he left North Carolina College in 1984. He is nicknamed 'Air' because of the amazing way he seems to hang in the air when taking a shot. He averaged over 32 points a game, season after season. In 1990 he scored 69 points in one game, playing for the Chicago Bulls against Cleveland. His 1986–7 season's total of 3041 points has only been beaten once, by the legendary Wilt Chamberlain in 1961–2.

The most successful point scorer is Lew Alcindor. This is not a famous name because in 1969 he became a Muslim and took the name Kareem Abdul-Jabbar. The following year he turned professional, and carried on playing for over twenty years. He played 1560 games in the NBA and ABA (American Basketball Association) leagues. He is still the highest ever career scorer with 38,387 points.

BASKETBALL FACTS

In the 1961–2 season Wilt Chamberlain had the NBA season's highest points per game average of 50.4, playing for Philadelphia. The following season he almost beat his record when playing for his new team of San Francisco.

Michael Jordan scoring a basket for the Bulls.

In today's professional game a player can earn recognition as the greatest of their time by winning the title of MVP (Most Valuable Player). The player who has won this title most often is Earvin Johnson, usually called 'Magic' Johnson. He won the MVP title in 1987, 1989 and 1990. Unlike most winners of this title Magic Johnson is a guard, not a forward or centre.

In 1992 and 1993 Fiona Murray of the Northampton 76ers was elected as the Woman Player of the Year by the English Basketball Association. She has been capped 51 times by England. The last time was in their historic away win over Bulgaria in January 1994. Fiona is one of the tallest players in the women's game in Britain at just over 1.93 m (6 ft 4 in).

Most professional basketball records have been broken in the last few years. However, in 1961 the graceful and agile centre, Bob Pettitt, set a single-game record of 19 free throws without missing, and this is still a record today.

Fiona Murray, the Woman Player of the Year in 1992 and 1993.

Famous teams

Perhaps the most famous basketball team ever is the Harlem Globetrotters. When its founder, Abe Saperstein, first took his all-black team on the road in 1927, a new era in the game was begun. Before this basketball had been a game for white college teams. The Globetrotters changed everything. At first they played exhibition matches in a Chicago ballroom. Then they went on the road, and all over the world. People flocked to see them wherever they went. They had TV specials on the major channels in countries they visited.

Michael Douglas of the Harlem Globetrotters making an athletic shot.

The Globetrotters were well known for their amazing ball-handling and their comedy routines. They could spin the ball on the end of their fingers, and could head the ball, or drop-kick it, into the basket. Everyone in the team seemed able to do behind-the-back dribbles and blind passing (passing to a team mate who was behind him). It looked so easy, but it took hours of dedicated practice. Their most famous player was 'Meadowlark' Lemon. He was well known for the dramatic way he would fall down when he had been fouled. The Globetrotters' matches abroad were always seen as entertainment and never taken too seriously – but they made sure they were so good that they always won.

Professional basketball began in the USA in 1898, but the National Basketball Association was not formed until the National Basketball League and the Basketball Association of America combined in 1949. The 27 teams in the NBA are divided into Eastern and Western Conferences. After the season of 82 games there is a play-off between the top eight teams in each Conference. The Conference champions play each other in a best-of-seven final for the NBA Championship. The Boston Celtics are the most successful team in the NBA, winning the championship sixteen times.

In the early 1960s Abe Saperstein, the Harlem Globetrotters' manager, fell out with the basketball league members of the NBA and tried to form a new league – the American Basketball League (ABL). Although he attracted many of the world's greatest players to join him, the league never gained enough interest and closed down in 1976.

The sport is thought of as new in the UK, but in 1986 the English Basketball Association celebrated its 50th anniversary. In the first National Championships, Hoylake YMCA beat London Polytechnic 32–31. The first televised game in the UK was in 1963, and the National League was formed in 1972. Many of the players had seen the Globetrotters on TV and wanted to play this exciting game. There are now thousands of clubs all over Europe, many of which are professional.

Kingston playing Manchester for the Natwest Trophy in 1990.

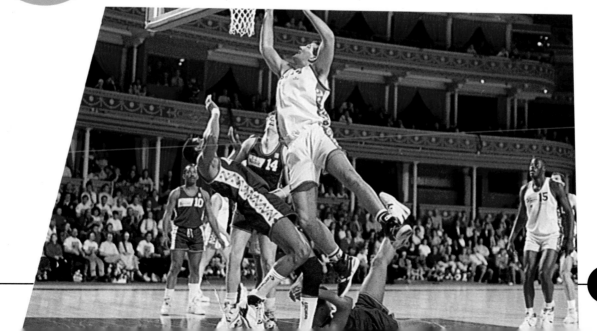

Basketball highlights

I f how much a player can earn in a season is a good way to decide how important a game is, then basketball appears to be incredibly important. In the 1991–2 season the Boston Celtics centre, Larry Bird, earned over $7 million. The average annual salary for an NBA professional was over one million dollars! The average height was over 2 m (6 ft 7 in) too. High earners in every way!

There can be no other sport where two people compete on equal terms despite a difference of 70 cm (2ft 6 in) between them. In the American professional league Tyrone Bogues is 1.6 m (5 ft 3 in) tall and Manute Bol 2.3 m (7 ft 7 in) tall!

In 1983, Detroit scored 186 points against Denver. This is the highest score ever recorded in the NBA.

Larry Bird in action.

The USSR playing Yugoslavia in the 1988 Olympics.

In the same game Denver scored 184, the second-highest score ever. The combined total of 370 points is unlikely ever to be beaten. At the end of the normal playing time the score was 145 all. It was still tied at the end of two five-minute periods of extra time. At the end of the third period of extra time Detroit were just ahead.

Over 200 million people paid to see games in the NBA leagues in 1993. This made basketball the most popular spectator sport in the USA. The smallest stadium, Salt Palace, in Utah holds only 12,616 when it is full. The largest capacity arena is the Louisiana Superdrome, which holds over 47,000.

The record for scoring 100 points in a professional game is held by Wilt Chamberlain, playing for Philadelphia against New York on 2 March 1962. He also scored over 70 points in six different games. No one else has ever achieved this.

Basketball in Britain and Europe is growing rapidly. October 1994 sees the first ever European All-Star game. The venue for the game will move all over Europe, so that as many fans as possible can see the great players joining up and showing how good they are.

Glossary

bounce pass A slow pass where the ball is propelled to a team mate by bouncing it on the floor.

centre line and **centre circle** The game is started by one member of each team standing in the circle, either side of the centre line, and jumping for the ball.

centres The tallest players, who play in and around the key and score from close range, also known as posts or pivots.

chest pass Fast, accurate pass at close range. Both hands hold the ball at chest level, then pass it by extending the arms and flicking the wrists and fingers.

dribble To move along the court bouncing the ball as you go.

drive Dribbling the ball towards the basket, trying to beat an opponent and take a shot.

dunk shot A spectacular one- or two-handed shot where the player takes the ball above the basket and pushes it down through the hoop.

forwards Tall players who can drive and shoot well and play close to the basket.

free throws Penalty shots taken from behind the free-throw line, worth one point if a basket is scored.

free-throw line The line on the court behind which penalty shots awarded for personal fouls are taken.

guards The smaller, faster players who bring the ball up the court and start attacks and draw defenders away from their basket.

hand-off pass When close together, one player throws the ball up and a team mate catches it.

held ball When two players from each team are holding the ball at the same time and neither of them can get it away easily.

hook-shot A one-handed shot from the side of the basket that is thrown by swinging the arm in a circle.

jump-ball A player from each team jumps for the ball after it is thrown up in the air by the referee to start the game.

jump-shot A one-handed shot where the ball is released at the top of a jump.

key or **three-second area** The keyhole-shaped area on the court between the baseline and the basket where an attacking player is allowed to stay for only three seconds.

lay-up shot A one-handed shot at the end of a run that is bounced into the basket off the backboard.

overhead pass The ball is held in both hands above the head and is flicked by wrists and fingers to a team mate.

personal foul A foul that involves contact with another player.

referee The senior official who, with the umpire, controls the game.

set shot A long-range shot from an almost stationary position. Used mostly for free throws.

technical foul A foul against the spirit of the game and which is unsporting.

three-point line A basket scored from outside this line on the court 6.25 m from the basket is worth three points.

time-out A break in play, called by the team coaches or the referee, that lasts up to one minute.

umpire The junior official who, with the referee, controls the game.

violation A foul that does not involve another player but breaks the rules.

Index